Ryan,

Thanks for

Parenting.
ALL Kids!

You are truly

Missed @
Nelson!

Best!!

Dr. Lane

Parenting Yesterday, Parenting Today

Is Technology the New Surrogate Parent?
A Psychological Perspective of Our Culturally
Diverse Society

Dr. S. Elaine Love

ISBN-13: 978-1500735555

DEDICATION

This book is dedicated to struggling parents

everywhere.

ACKNOWLEDGEMENTS

With great appreciation, I wish to thank my mother and sister for supporting me through all of my endeavors over the years. I would like to express my sincere gratitude to my loving husband Thomas James and my amazing daughter Asya Love for being a fabulous family. Thank you to my godsisters, Pastor Jennifer and Helen L. Edwards, for always believing in me. Many thanks to my 104 year old grandmother Sarah, who is alive and well today, my grandmother, the late Clotilda Marerro, and mis tías (my aunts) for being great role models.

I would like to gratefully acknowledge Dr. Merri Rieger—EVERY Child, EVERY Day— Dr. Tammy Campbell for your inspiration, and Randy Matheson for being a great coach.

This book is in memory of my father whose life was cut short during a difficult era in which he grew up, and whose life struggles ended up being mine. But his vision for our family and others to overcome adversity is the work that will continue now and for generations to come.

Most of all, I thank my heavenly Father, who continues to give me the inspiration, strength, motivation, and desire to help others.

FORWARD

Dr. Elaine Love has been a role model for educators and parents for over 20 years. During this time, she has worn many hats—school counselor, college professor, PhD program advisor, and school administrator. As a parent, she has raised a daughter who is flourishing. Dr. Love brings solid credentials, a deep understanding of different cultures, and a wealth of experience to her current position as an administrator in a large, diverse middle school. It is, however, her deep commitment to leadership through service that makes her shine and makes the insights on parenting she shares in this book so timely.

As educators and parents, we live in difficult times. Families are changing, classrooms are changing, and technology has become a major influence in children's lives—an influence which tests the abilities of parents to mold the character and integrity of their sons and daughters. *Parenting Yesterday, Parenting Today* gives parents a vehicle for exploring their parenting styles. It identifies the moral dilemmas parents grapple with, and outlines pragmatic solutions to the problems they face. This book offers parents sound advice for working with educators, not only to advocate for their children, but to understand best practices for raising them.

Parenting Yesterday, Parenting Today is a book that should be read reflectively. Take time to think about and answer the questions at the end of each section before going on to the next. Create time for yourself, as busy as your life is, to meditate about what you are doing well and what you would like to improve about your parenting. Raising children is a

journey full of both golden moments and miss-steps.

Use this book to acknowledge your parenting

strengths, and use Dr. Love's advice and advocacy to

grow as a parent.

— Patricia Cribb-Baskin, Teacher

TABLE OF CONTENTS

INTRODUCTION

Parenting Yesterday, Parenting Today is a look at where we've been as parents in the past and where we are going as a society today. It is clear that parenting yesterday was very different than today, so what can we do as a society or as parents to work within the parameters of today's expectations and guidelines, while still keeping our morals and values high and our families intact?

The demand of parenting continues to increase in our world. These expectations add to the work for today's parents, who are busier than ever, working both in and outside the home. While daily demands are not going away, parents are called upon daily to make their best judgments when it comes to their children. Complicated as modern parenting is, there is no one recipe or manual with ALL of the answers for PARENTS. I write this book, however, in support of parents who need a few more ideas on how to take time to shape today's children in such a busy, demanding, and competitive world, with technology at the helm of it all.

Keeping our children safe was not an easy task yesterday, nor is it any easier today. Parents are unable to be with their child 24/7, so we can only train them to the best of our ability to be good and honest citizens and hope those skills will shine and steer them from the lure of peer pressure or the many negative aspects of our society. We often know that some of our kids will choose to make poor decisions when we are not around, which is to be expected, but we hope this will occur less often.

As I write this book, remembering all of the experiences, stories, and journeys that took me so many places, all of the events and conversations that helped me understand my trials and tribulations as a kid, I reflected the reasons why my parents made the decisions they did for our family. I appreciate how, no matter what, they kept our family appropriate for our family values intact. Their decisions helped me to establish my family values when I became a parent. Then, I think how the next generation always wants to do better than the last.

I write this book for the parents I've worked with over the years who struggled with, "Now that my child has made the wrong decision. For that reason, it is important to have positive family values to counteract the negative influences our kids are exposed to daily, but good positive family values will overpower them. And for those of you who may not have created a positive family environment, or don't know where to begin, then my hope is that, after you take this journey, you will be able to create one.

CHAPTER 1: PARENTING

Parenting: The Beginning

Choosing to become a parent and to be responsible for another human being is one of the biggest life-changing decisions you will ever encounter. There are plenty of books and literature available for expectant mothers and fathers. Some parents choose to be prepared and read books that share the size of the fetus, what to expect each month during the pregnancy, and how an expectant mother can stay healthy. Books and literature also share what to expect the first few years in life. There are excellent materials available to prepare parents from zero to birth, age one, the terrible twos, and maybe a few more years, but what happens when the children enter pre-school? As a parent, do you continue to seek out literature for the elementary years, middle school years, and high school or beyond?

Yesterday's and today's parents may have chosen to rely on others' experiences or rely on their own best judgment. Parents today are busier than ever and are out in the workforce more than yesterday's parents. Since not as much time is allotted to educating children at home, when children attend a formal educational setting this responsibility is now transferred to the schools. Educating yourself as a parent about best practices in parenting can be another powerful tool that aids in the success of your child.

What Is parenting?

In the last century, parenting was described as to be or act as a mother or father "taking care of children until they are old enough to take care of themselves." A parent can also be described as one who gives birth to or nurtures and raises a child.

Today, should these definitions change or remain the same? What are the factors that change the face of parenting? Does your cultural background determine your parenting style? In our changing world, to meet the needs of our diverse society, should we redefine parenting? I propose the responsibility of parenting falls on the shoulders of ALL adults who come in contact with children. Regardless of whether one has given birth or not, a parent can be any respectful adult who is there to mentor, guide, and provide the basic necessities for a child. Any adult who makes good decisions, shares good times and bad, is a shoulder to cry on, models right from wrong so a child can become a productive, contributing member of society is parenting. How would you define parenting?

What Does Parenting Look Like Today?

Today, we are in a society in which parenting looks very different from long ago. Some will argue that grandparents are the primary parents today. Why? Because, in some cases it appears that grandparents are the ones providing the most stable and safest environment for children.

My Grandparents

Growing up in Brooklyn, New York in the 1960s and 1970s, various events in my life required me to live with my grandparents off and on, on a temporary basis. Each time it was the best decision for my family. Later in Chapter 6, you will understand better why. Living with my grandmother ("Mi' abuela" in Spanish), I had the opportunity to embrace and love her just as much as my parents. She shared great stories with me, and I was able to enjoy our conversations in "Spanglish." There are many moments with her that I will always treasure.

Diverse Parents

Today, we are a diverse society, and our families reflect this diversity. Regardless of race, creed, or color, people from every walk of life fill the role of parent. Some kids may have parents of the same gender, while others may have parents of a different race. Does it matter? My family was a very diverse family of different races. I would argue that it does not matter as long as there is love and a healthy and positive environment, which was very obvious in my family.

While today our families are more diverse than ever, they are often more nuclear than in the past. This is why, as a society, it is important for ALL of us to play a positive role in shaping the development of children. As in years gone by, teachers, coaches, friends, family members, and mentors interact with our kids on a daily basis, but in many cases their influence is more deeply felt, given the time constraints so many parents struggle with.

Today's family is very creative. From both parents, to single parents, to foster care, to having grandparents as guardians, someone is required to do the parenting. That said, as parents, are we really providing for our kids' needs to the best of our ability?

Influential Teachers in My Life

Relationships can shape people in a positive or negative way. During my elementary years, I truly enjoyed ALL of my teachers. By the time I reached middle school, my English teacher and band teacher chose to be my mentors. They chose me; I didn't choose them. I didn't understand why, but maybe these teachers saw something important in me that I didn't see in myself. They demonstrated that they valued me as a human being because they took the time to get to know me. This really made all of the difference in the world. Going with these teachers to the Empire State Building, the Statue of Liberty, Radio City Music Hall, and museums on field trips made our relationship even stronger and broadened my horizons. They helped me to believe that I could be anything I chose to be. They took time to understand my thoughts and dreams, and they encouraged me in the career I decided I would venture into when I became an adult.

Do you remember growing up with teachers, coaches, and relatives who were very influential in your life? Besides your parents, did these people play a key role in helping to shape your life today? Regardless, would you consider a teacher, a coach, or a mentor important in your child's life?

Parenting Reflection Journal:
Influential People

Other than your parents, who was the most influential person in your life?

_____
_____
_____

Did this influential person change your life?

_____
_____
_____

If you did not have an influential person in your life, would you have preferred to have had one?

_____
_____
_____

Is there an influential person in your child(ren)'s life?

_____
_____
_____

If not, will you consider helping your child(ren) to find one?

_____
_____
_____

CHAPTER 2: PARENTING STYLES

Which Style Matches You or Your Parent(s)?

Have you ever wondered if parents learned their skills from their own parents? In some cases it is apparent, and in others cases it is a mystery. Learning parenting from our parents and mimicking their style exactly could mean that you have conditioned yourself to do so. This is just an example of human beings following a habit they have learned or seen in their environment. Do you remember learning in school about the famous psychologist Ivan Pavlov? He conditioned a dog to salivate and expect food when he rang a bell. Well, as you can see in humans, if someone consistently has you follow the same expectations, whether right or wrong, or act without thinking about reasons or consequences, you become conditioned to do that behavior. Recognizing that you have been conditioned and that you are an unhealthy product of your environment is the first step to breaking the cycle of ineffective parenting. On the other hand, have you considered conditioning or helping your children to form good habits such as doing their homework, taking out the garbage, or cleaning their room? Our parents conditioned us to do things their way, without our knowledge. As parents, we can mindfully condition our children to have habits which will create positive outcomes in their lives. Regardless of your parenting style, you can use conditioning to train your kids. Let's look at what the four styles of parenting developed by well-known therapist Dianna Baumrind.

Authoritarian Parenting Style

The authoritarian parent is characterized as a parent with high expectations of compliance and conformity to parental rules and directions. For the most part, kids of some of these parents will live in fear. In some cases, they may not know what to expect because of the inconsistency in discipline. These parents may believe in the idea of "spare the rod, spoil the child." Children will have difficulties opening up and sharing with this type of parent. This parenting style could cause some kids to defy authority or be duly influenced by society. Particularly later in life, this child can end up having difficulties with respecting authority figures.

Permissive Parenting Style

The next style of parenting is the permissive style of parenting. This type of parent is characterized as the warm and fuzzy type of parent, who is able to develop a strong parent and child relationship. ALL the friends of children raised by this type of parent love to hang out with both parent and child because they know that this parent will allow a lot of freedom with little or no rules to follow. Permissive parents are afraid to make demands or hold their children accountable in fear that the children will not be happy with them. These parents will also allow their children to run their own program and makes excuses for them to avoid disciplinary actions. In this parenting style, children simply learn how to blame someone else for their shortcomings, even if the children themselves are at fault.

Authoritative Parenting Style

This type of parent has high expectations for their child's behavior, but this style allows for the child to have conversations with their parents about those expectations. These parents teach their child about cause and effect, decision making, and self-sufficiency. They raise their children to be successful, articulate, happy with themselves, and generous to others. These children end up being liked and respected by their peers, and well-rounded as adults.

Neglectful Parenting Style & Technology

This style of parenting is similar to the permissive style, but without much interaction between parent and child. This parent provides food, shelter, and clothing, but emotionally may be uninvolved in their child's life. In this type of situation the child could have some serious and negative issues going on outside of the home, but the neglectful parent may not be aware of it unless they hear from the neighbors, the police, or the school. In some cases, later in life these children may end up resenting their parents. Baurmind added this fourth style much later in her study of parenting to reflect the changes in our society. We see this style being used more and more in our families today, since the use of technology is steadily increasing. It appears

that technology is becoming a surrogate parent.

Harmonious Parenting Style

In addition to these four parenting styles, Dr. Stephen Greenspan, a well-known clinical professor of Psychiatry and Pediatrics at George Washington University Medical School, added a new model he calls "Harmonious Parenting." His purpose was to address the needs of children in our current, diverse society. In this style, parents are in tune with their child and use their high level of awareness to seek ways to accept, respect, and understand their children to allow a certain level of autonomy. In this style, norms and rules are established for both child and parent, and ALL are harmonious and accepting. These parents tend to meet the needs of their children quickly. They normally know what is going on with their children, and they will typically involve them in a lot of positive, and sometimes expensive, types of activities, such as elite sports, piano lessons, band, orchestra, art, or other activities their children express an interest in. These children normally end up highly successful in life.

My Family's Parenting Style

As a child, my mother exhibited the authoritative style of parenting, while my father was the authoritarian type of parent. How confusing this was for me as a child! I always feared my father growing up. After my father passed away when I was in middle school (see chapter 3), my mother's style of parenting dominated. My mother, who grew up on the Island of Puerto Rico, learned from her family's culture to embrace the authoritative parenting style, which was typical to families on the island during that era. My mother learned early in her life how to be very self-sufficient, generous, and responsible. She quickly learned cause and effect. This style is the one I was conditioned to, and it became my primary way of parenting as a mother. If my father had been alive throughout my high school years, would I have

adopted my mother's authoritative style or would I

have favored my father's?

My Combination Parenting Style

Regardless of my past, having understood these styles, and wanting to change my style to match today's changing world, I became more of the authoritative/harmonious type parent. The combination of these styles allowed me to interact with my child quite often and work with her on being a respectful and a responsible person. Supporting and guiding her in school and all of her positive activities such as ballet, pageants, sports, and lots of community service projects, encouraged her self-esteem and independence, and motivated her to leave the nest right after high school to attend college.

Technology & Your Parenting Style

As parents, we must recognize our parenting style and own it. In households where there are two parents with different styles, it is obvious that these styles can affect our children positively or negatively. The key is to be consistent. Also, be present. Don't allow technology to raise your kids. Understanding and knowing your parenting style is the beginning of taking control as a parent, and using technology responsibly will avoid having it take over the parenting role. Technology is not an effective surrogate parent. Preparing kids for the real world can be accomplished through positive, supportive family relationships.

Remember, your parenting has an important impact on our child's development. Think about what type of impact you want to have in molding and developing your child. It's never too late to sharpen your parenting skills. If you need help, consider resources in your community, such as parenting classes, which can truly have a positive impact on you and your child.

Parenting Reflection Journal:
Parenting Styles

Which parenting style best describes your parent(s)?

_____

_____

_____

Which parenting style best describes you?

_____

_____

_____

Do you as a parent exhibit a combination of two
parenting styles according to your mood or stress
level?

_____

_____

_____

With technology increasing in today's society, are
these traditional parenting styles still as prevalent
today as they were yesterday?

_____

_____

_____

How will you use your parenting style to positively affect your child(ren)'s success?

_____

_____

_____

What will you do as a parent to exhibit appropriate and consistent parenting styles?

_____

_____

_____

How will you encourage open dialogue with your child(ren) about family expectations?

_____

_____

_____

_____

_____

_____

_____

_____

_____

_____

_____

_____

_____

_____

CHAPTER 3: SINGLE PARENTING YESTERDAY, SINGLE PARENTING TODAY

It is fairly simple to understand that the definition of single parenting is one adult being responsible for rearing the child(ren). Single parenting is nothing new in this day and age, but we are seeing an increase. Why? The numerous factors include rises in divorce, illnesses, drugs, jail, violence, and crime. The impact of these changes is a society dealing with the aftermath of children being left behind. Some of our children are witnessing or dealing with violence in their families. How does our society support these children in need? If we do not help, success often will be unobtainable for these children and they can easily end up on a negative path.

Who Are Our Single Parents?

Today, our single parents are from all walks of life. We are seeing more and more fathers in the role of single parenting. As well, single parents are often foster parents, grandparents, or other family members.

Is Single Parenting Easy?

Single parenting has its ups and downs, just like anything else in life. It can be overwhelming, and it requires good organizational skills in order to meet the demands of the entire family. Using Sundays to plan, prepare, and pre-cook meals for the workweek can help to save you time and energy. Assigning a schedule of chores to all family members can aid in creating a less stressful and hectic environment, and at the same time it teaches children responsibility. Scheduling time for children to complete homework, maybe right after school so they can enjoy the rest of their evening and/or complete chores, can create more time for the family to spend together. Creating a weekly schedule that is right for your family is yet another way to create less stress in an organized single parent household. What would your family

plan look like?

Single Parenting: Don't Turn Your Child into the ABSENT PARENT

While single parenting can be very busy, it is important to allow children to enjoy their years as children. Unconsciously, some parents will turn their child into the absent parent. Remember, your child still needs the opportunity to enjoy childhood. Although your child can be responsible for assisting in some of the daily activities in the household, it is unfair to place children in a parenting role. A mother should not turn her son into an absent dad for the other siblings, and neither should a father turn his oldest daughter into the missing mother. Being role models or leaders for the younger siblings, however, is very appropriate. Having children take on additional roles can only lead to resentment and confusion, and could hinder them from becoming

productive members of society.

Life Changes: Now I Am Growing Up in a Single Parent Environment

In the previous chapter, I shared the two different parenting styles I experienced growing up. By the time I reached middle school, a violent tragedy left me with only one parent. What happened? Leaving Brooklyn, New York for a road trip with my parents to Florida in 1967, a stop at a restaurant in South Carolina forever changed our lives. During those times, a restaurant could refuse to serve a person food based on the color of his or her skin. When my father figured this out at the restaurant and then tried to walk away to avoid an argument, he was shot several times, and I had the first-hand experience of seeing the blood. Quickly, I learned at the age of six the definition of the word prejudice. My father survived, but suffered complications from the incident for the rest of his life, and he ultimately passed away when I was in middle school.

Sadly enough, individual counseling or a support group was not recommended for me. This only made it easy for me to internalize everything in life and not experience emotions. Seeing tragedies became no big deal in my life. The lack of some type of assistance can do that to you. This incident had the potential to help or hinder my upbringing and, subsequently, my life as an adult. Instead, I chose to use this as a way to build strength by keeping busy participating in church, a number of sports, pageants, and community events. I decided to overcome my barriers and use this tragedy and not turn it into an excuse. I chose to use this negative experience as a pathway to growth. My family, mentors, and teachers, as well as other community members, were very instrumental in shaping my life.

That's my story. Do you have a story? If so, are you using it as an excuse or are you using it as a way to grow and soar like an eagle? As a society, how can we help our kids today overcome trauma or other negative life experiences?

Parenting Reflection Journal:
Single Parenting

How can you alleviate the stress in a single parent household?

_____
_____
_____

How can you avoid turning your child(ren) into an ABSENT PARENT?

_____
_____
_____

Do you have family support or extended family? If not, who could be your support?

_____
_____
_____

What is your single parent organizational plan? How will the child(ren) help? What expectations will you assign family members?

_____
_____
_____
_____
_____
_____

Parenting Reflection Journal:
Overcoming Life Tragedies

Think about the tragedies our children are dealing with today and how they change family dynamics. Are more children today dealing with their own tragedies?

_____
_____
_____
_____
_____

Can outside resources such as counseling and support groups assist? If so, do you know where to seek help?

_____
_____
_____
_____
_____

How can we create opportunities for our children to use even their most negative experiences as a pathway to growth?

_____
_____
_____
_____
_____

CHAPTER 4: TECHNOLOGY, THE NEW SURROGATE PARENT?

Technology today is used for many positive things in our society. It truly makes our world go around. What about technology use amongst today's youth? Our youth use it to complete research papers and learn more about our changing world. There is no argument here: technology can help them grow academically. But what about socially? Do we inadvertently use technology to babysit our youth? Is this a good substitute for family time instead of enjoying the great outdoors together? Are we having meaningful conversations with our youth? Are most of today's youth able to have meaningful conversations or write complete sentences that are grammatically correct? As a society, we must look at the long-term effect of technology.

Technology: The New Babysitter

In the past, it appeared that the television was the best babysitter available. It kept kids quiet and occupied for hours, and you, as a parent, may have been able to have some quiet time. Now technology appears to be the new and improved babysitter. With parents being busier than ever trying to meet the high demands of work and society, something is sacrificed. What did our parents do long ago to avoid missing out on family time? Have we forgotten? Was that so long ago? How do we get back family time and connect emotionally with our children?

Back to the Basics: Let's Connect With Our Kids Emotionally, Not Electronically

Connecting with our youth emotionally, allowing for family time, and limiting the use of electronics can only help our youth to become well-rounded and prepared for society. Are our youth today obsessed by technology? Do machines mean more to our kids than anything in the world?

Those of us who took psychology at school remember learning about Maslow's Hierarchy of Needs. Some of these needs include self-actualization, esteem, love/belonging, and safety. These were the basic needs then, should they be changed now? Technology was not as pervasive during that time. Should we change it today? Does it need to be listed as one of the basic needs? In our families today we must decide how much we really

NEED to use technology in our household.

Parenting Reflection Journal:
Technology

Do you have meaningful conversations with your child(ren)? What topics do you share with your child(ren)?

_____
_____
_____

Do you monitor your family's electronics, etc. in your household?

_____
_____
_____

What does family time look like in your household?

_____
_____
_____

Does your family spend time enjoying the great outdoors together? If not, what activities would you like to do?

_____
_____
_____
_____
_____
_____

CHAPTER 5: SOCIAL MEDIA

Today, youth learn a great deal from SOCIAL MEDIA. It appears that electronic communication is used by an enormous percentage of our society. While electronic communication can be a quicker way to communicate, it is not a good medium to foster the emotional and social aspects of our children's development. It appears that we are losing our youth to an obsession with social media.

Does social media teach our youth how to build positive relationships? In some cases, our youth have shown an increase in using profanity openly in public, in texts, in schools, around adults, and on social media. What happened to those days when we did not openly use profanity and it was done in a quiet manner not for ALL to hear? In the past if an adult witnessed such type of behavior they would chastise the child for using the language and in some cases they would report it to the child's parent. Those days weren't that long ago. We as parents have to think about the root cause and put a plug in it. Are we allowing too much freedom to our children? How can our youth learn to function socially and in a professional manner in the real world?

Some of our kids today are lacking social skills, and this is showing to be a huge problem in our society. Kids text grammatically incorrect words, and this is not helpful in preparing them for the world of work. Technology certainly cannot replace relationships, so how do we balance the two effectively for our youth? As parents we have to sharpen our skills and recognize what our kids need to function in this world positively. Without good skills, how will our youth know how to interview for a job or communicate with employers? Is social media crippling the development of our youth? Are the lives of our youth really improved by access to technology?

Parents' Perspectives About Social Media

In my discussion with a few parents about how social media affected the upbringing of their children I received some very insightful feedback. One parent's perspective is:

> If kids are to become more engaged in living productive lives instead of watching it pass them by, then there would be less time for social media to take over. Fostering high self-esteem is one of the very best gifts a parent can give a child. Then, they are more apt to become movers and shakers who value technology without making it the dominant part of their lives.
>
> —Y.S.N.

Another parent shared how technology is used differently because they are a family of five. The children include a thirteen-year-old daughter, an eleven-year-old daughter, and a four-year-old son. Both parents agreed that they did not want their children to be influenced by social media and technology. The family are not Facebookers, tweeters, or instagramers. They are aware that there is a lot of uncensored information out there as well as predators, and they do not want their children to have this exposure. These parents are firm believers in saying "no" to their children. They have conversations with their children about the positive and negative aspects of social media and technology, and are not afraid to say "no".

They said there are good things that can be done with social media and technology as well as bad; however, we tell our kids, "You are not getting one [a smart phone], so stop asking." Their children do not have smart phones; in fact, two of their daughters share a phone that allows "texting" only.

It's from 2009. The mother is the parent in the family who checks the phone to see what the children "text" and the content of their conversations. Also, she reminds them that she can get anything the children delete from their phone from Verizon at any time.

The parents keep the lines of communication open so their children can feel free to talk with them about their concerns, needs, and wants. The parents are always open to listening and hearing their thoughts and opinions. The parents allow the children to use technology when it pertains to homework, and they feel that this is enough for them.

—R.B.

Another parent gave me feedback about her experiences having an older child, who is now 33, and a younger child, now 14. This parent has experienced, first hand, parenting with and without access to the internet. She allows her younger child to check grades or do homework, but does not allow access to any social media.

—A.S.

Parenting Reflection Journal:
Technology & Social Media

How much access does your child(ren) have to social media?

_____

_____

_____

Do you monitor your child(ren)'s social media sites? If so, is everything on their site or coming into their site appropriate?

_____

_____

_____

What can you do as a parent to avoid cyberbullying on social media?

_____

_____

_____

Have you and your child(ren) signed a SOCIAL MEDIA CONTRACT that speaks to professionalism and responsibly on social media?

_____

_____

_____

Social Media Contract

I, _____ will show appropriateness and professionalism on social media, such as Facebook, texts, chatrooms, Instagram, and any other sites which my parents and the public will be able to view. Sharing anything inappropriate can affect my character and reputation, as well as cause long-term effects. If I have any issues with negative social media at any time I will discuss these issues with my parents.

Child's Signature _____

Parent's Signature_____

CHAPTER 6: EMBRACING YOUR CULTURE

Today our world is more diverse than ever. Although diversity is increasingly common, some of our youth of mixed race are still having difficulties embracing their own culture because they are not accepted by their peers. Some will strongly choose one culture over the other instead of balancing them both, but how can they balance them both when the parent from one culture is absent? Those youth who are unable to fit in may choose to isolate themselves, and this can hinder the development of good social skills. We must find ways for kids who are from several different cultures to receive respect and embrace all different types of cultures. What can we do as a community to help our students embrace their cultures regardless of an absent parent?

Embracing My Culture

While I was growing up in Brooklyn, New York, diversity was rich, respected, and embraced. Later, when I left New York to relocate to Florida I had a totally different experience. There I experienced the feeling of isolation because, according to my peers, I looked different. My Puerto Rican culture and ability to speak Spanish was something difficult for some to understand. Maybe I looked a little different than most on the outside, but on the inside I was still a respectful, responsible, and generous person. Why was that not enough?

My mother and I did not discuss this, so I thought it was normal for my peers to name-call about the complexion of my skin or the different language I spoke. I assumed that if you look different than most, then isolation was to be expected. By the time I reached high school, I finally figured it out that this was not normal and this behavior from my peers was not okay. In learning to embrace the skin I am in, it was helpful to connect with my family and teachers, who would frequently remind me that it is okay to be different. Participating in a wealth of activities that embraced diversity was also helpful in my development.

Kids today may not have very many people to check in with because they look different. Some may not feel comfortable sharing with parents or teachers the negative attitudes they are getting from their peers. Often, some kids have the opportunity in their writing class to write about their culture. This is a great way for kids to connect with others, learn about themselves, and become comfortable in the skin they are in. Writing activities about my family and culture were very important and helpful for me in my upbringing and deflected the attitudes of those who judged me for the way I look or talk. I learned to ignore the negativity and like who I am regardless of what others say.

Here is an example of a writing activity in the form of a poem that helped me to like me. It is called "Where I Am From," which was adapted from George Ella Lyon.

Where I Am From

I am from a city that never sleeps.

"If you can make it there, you can make it anywhere."

I am from a culture where Coney Island was my personal playground.

I am from a neighborhood mixed with Blacks, Whites, Puerto Ricans, Jews, and Italians.

I am from a culture in which it was mandatory to wear a dog tag to and from school with your name and address on it, just in case you got lost.

I am from Boricua, Puerto Rican Flag, and Salsa Dancing.

I am from a culture that by age nine, I would catch the subway or city bus alone to get to and from school.

I am from a culture in which I had to miss school to take Mi' Abuela to her appointments on the subway and translated her needs since she didn't speak English.

I am from a culture where I was a straight "A" student, and when I missed school, the teachers would ask, "Where were you? We missed you." But I was too embarrassed to tell them why.

I am from a culture where the best getaways were Far Rockaway Beach, ice skating at Rockefeller Center, touring the Statue of Liberty, and the Macy's Thanksgiving Day Parade.

I am from handball, double Dutch, and making go carts.

I am from a culture of Farina, bacalao, plantains, pasteles, knishes, matzo balls, warm roasted chestnuts, toasted bread dunked in coffee milk, and canned Goya products.

I am from a culture of taking Mi' Abuela to Catholic Church for Spanish Mass, and after church making homemade bread with her.

I am from the reason why I spent so much time with Mi' Abuela because in 1967, when I was age six tragedy would strike, and my father would pass away.

I am from a culture where by age six,
I learned the hard way about RACISM and some people may not like you because of the color of your skin.

I am from a culture where I often stated to myself, "What a way for a six year old to learn about RACISM, can someone please explain?"

I am from a culture that I must say thanks to those teachers who mentored me; I was able to receive athletic and pageant scholarships, which helped me to get where I am today.

I was able to heal and let go of the anger from that tragedy that occurred in my past in order to move forward and onward.

I am from a culture that now I have helped myself, it is important for me to help others, especially our kids today because they may be going through their OWN TRAGEDY TOO.

That's Where I'm From
Where Are You From?

Helping Our Kids to Connect Culturally

Helping our kids to connect culturally is not an easy job. Parents, teachers, family, and community members can play a key role in helping our youth today with this challenge. These connections can only help our youth to embrace their diversity and feel good about the skin they are in. It is a basis for kids having a positive attitude about themselves as well as others. As a parent, think of ways to help your kids connect positively with their culture(s) as well as with others, even if there is a missing parent.

Parenting Reflection Journal:
Embracing Your Culture

Are you comfortable with the skin you are in? Are your children?

_____

_____

How can we help our kids to be culturally connected?

_____

_____

_____

What can we ALL do if there is an absent parent and a child finds it difficult to connect to the missing parent's culture?

_____

_____

_____

Does/Do your child(ren) feel comfortable sharing how they feel about how they are treated because of their culture?

_____

_____

_____

Have you taken your child(ren) to any cultural events? If not, can you think of some that could benefit your family?

_____

_____

_____

Parenting Reflection Journal:
Where I Am From Poem Questions

What are some of your family values?

_____

_____

_____

What are some of your favorite family foods?

_____

_____

_____

What are your favorite activities?

_____

_____

_____

What did you and your family do for fun?

_____

_____

_____

Is there anything you remember about your family
that you still think about today?

_____

_____

_____

Parenting Reflection Journal:
Where I Am From Poem

_____
_____
_____
_____
_____
_____
_____
_____
_____
_____
_____
_____
_____
_____
_____
_____
_____
_____
_____
_____
_____
_____
_____
_____
_____

That's Where I'm From
Where Are You From?

CHAPTER 7: HOW ARE PARENTS DEALING WITH SCHOOLS TODAY?

Today, parents are busier than ever when it comes to working with schools in order to seek out the best education for their student. Certainly, much has changed over the years, but one thing that is still the same is the need to provide the best education for today's youth. Of course reading, writing, arithmetic, art, music, and physical education are still just as important today as they were in the past. One might wonder if the delivery in services is different today. Should the way we parent our children be different too?

Bridging the Gap Between Parents & Schools: Parent/School Communication 101

How can parents bridge the gap between school and home? In order for this connection to be implemented both the parents and the schools must work together positively. Therefore, there must be good effort from both parties for the sake of our kids. Parents, when it comes to communicating with schools, remember that today communication can be done in various ways, such as emails, phone calls, school messenger, or grades online. This type of technology works well for some parents, but for those who need more of a physical contact, such as a school visit, there are a few key tips one should follow.

Regardless of how the communication takes place, the positive relationship between the parent and school will be key. Parents who are unable to meet during parent and teacher conferences due to their work commitments should look at alternative ways to communicate with the school. Growing up, my mother's work schedule was very demanding, so written communication from the school, such as a progress report, note from the teacher, or a report card was her preference for connecting. Please note that some parents may not choose to communication at all because they don't know how to connect with the schools and English may not be their first language, so understanding the expectations of the school could be difficult for them. Regardless, there are ways for schools to communicate with these families through the use of technology, as well as home visits from school officials.

Basic Rules to Follow When Visiting Schools

Some parents may not have had the opportunity to read a book on basic rules to follow when visiting schools. Since it is not "rocket science," it is easy to assume that if you make an appointment to visit your doctor's office or dentist office that you should do the same when visiting the school, unless it is an emergency.

Using Your Problem-Solving Skills

Some of us have learned techniques for solving problems. These skills can be used in dealing with issues at school or any other situation. These are the basic steps for problem solving: 1) Define the problem; 2) Develop a plan; 3) Implement the plan; 4) Evaluate the results, and if the issue is not resolved then; 5) Go back through the process until the issue is resolved. Following these steps and interacting positively with the school can help with the success of your child.

Parent Expectations When Visiting Schools

While the relationship between parent and school is very important, the way we project ourselves as parents at the school is equally important. Here are some tips for parents to follow:

1) Be professional. When visiting the school, regardless what's going on, it is important for you to put your best foot forward. Whatever behavior we choose to model, remember our kids are like sponges and they will mimic our behavior and adopt our attitude.

2) Show respect. If you show disrespect to staff members at school, you are unconsciously giving permission for your child to disrespect the staff too. This could affect them throughout their education. Remember it is important to respect each

other. There is an old saying to "treat others like you would like to be treated." Remember karma has a way of coming back on you when you continually exhibit anger, disrespect, and unprofessionalism to others.

3) Keep the lines of communication open. Regardless what walk of life we are from, as parents we need to keep the lines of communication open and work positively with school officials. If you close your line of communication with the school, you will not be able to advocate for your child successfully. As well, your child will not be open to communicating with teachers and other staff.

4) Find a key person to connect with at the school. Having a go to person at the school will contribute to your child's success.

5) Listen to school officials. Before you choose sides, be sure to investigate as thoroughly as possible, prior to bringing the issues to the school. Do not assume the worst of the school or the situation. While we love to believe everything our children share with us and want to trust that they tell us the truth at all times, don't always assume that the school is wrong prior to hearing the school's side of the story. Remember, your kids are kids, and when they find themselves in a dilemma, they will try their best to get out of it. For the most part, school officials will be honest about what happened. They do not usually have a reason to be less than honest. While it is important for parents to listen to their child, it is also important for their well-being to get to the bottom of a troubling situation in order to foster growth and

accountability. Remember, we were kids once, and sometimes we were less than honest to our parents.

6) Get involved. There are many fascinating activities going on in schools. Do you know what they are? Check online to research such information. Ask your child if they received the school's newsletter via munchkin mail, since it will list activities that are going on at the school. Some schools will host literacy nights, curriculum nights, parent nights, family nights, cultural potlucks, math nights, talent shows, dances, community outreach events, sporting events, and Parent-Teacher-Student Association (PTSA) events. Although some of your kids will say it is not necessary for you to attend, the parents who attend anyway will discover how much fun these events can be. Participation in these

activities as parents can help us change our perspective and form a connection with the school, which is all part of building positive relationships.

7) As a parent, be empowered. Don't let someone take your power. Things do not have to be done out of anger all of the time. Anger doesn't solve anything. Be empowered, empower others, and show the schools that a resolution can occur in a professional manner. "Never let them see you sweat." In the scheme of things, our ultimate goal is to help our youth be all that they can be with support from school and home. This is one of the ultimate ways that parents can influence student success.

Parenting Reflection Journal:
School Success

What type of relationship do you have with your child(ren)'s school?

_____

_____

_____

_____

How can you deal positively with the school?

_____

_____

_____

_____

Is there a key person you can connect with at the school such as a school counselor, teacher, or principal?

_____

_____

_____

_____

Have you asked the school for assistance for your child(ren)?

_____

_____

_____

_____

How can you be empowered in your child(ren)'s education?

_____

_____

_____

_____

Do you plan on getting involved in any school activities?

_____

_____

_____

_____

CHAPTER 8: NOW YOUR KIDS ARE IN HIGH SCHOOL, WHAT'S NEXT?

Most parents understand that the elementary years are very precious. Maybe you spent time dropping kids off at school or picking them up. Maybe you participated in the PTSA to show support. You found all types of activities to get involved in at the school because you wanted to support your children in their early years. You helped with homework, and you called the teacher if you did not understand the assignments. You asked for assistance if needed. Then, your children went on to middle school, and you noticed that it was a bit more challenging. You needed more assistance from the school, and while you did your best to communicate with the school, sometimes you were frustrated. You did your best to help your children through the middle school years, and you and the school did what you could to mold them to be good citizens. Finally, they are ready to go off to high school. What's next? Hang in there parents. Your children still need you.

Have you checked the high school program to see what they offer? Have you been having conversations with your children since middle school to get an indication about what direction they are considering going in high school and about their future plans? Did you ever work with your children on journaling their future plans at an early age and investigate trends and anticipated job market needs for when they complete high school? These conversations should not only begin in high school, but should start early in middle school. Your children's school careers will go by so quickly.

Having these conversations all along can help your children to be one step further in deciding what courses will be beneficial for them in high school.

Parenting Reflection Journal:
Plans for the Future?

How should I prepare my child(ren) for preschool?

_____

_____

_____

How should I prepare my child(ren) for elementary school?

_____

_____

_____

Career discussion in middle school:
Fall_____

_____

_____

Spring_____

_____

_____

Field trips to different types of business:

_____

_____

_____

CHAPTER 9: KID, LET'S TALK ABOUT YOUR FUTURE ENDEAVORS

Parents, you have done everything humanly possible to support your child through the education process, but you were so busy working that you may not have shown much of a focus about your kid's next steps. Is it too late? It is not too late, but it may require more work for you and your child to figure out what comes next. Weighing your options by researching trends; visiting with career counselors; checking out colleges and their requirements; visiting vocational schools; and investigating the military, businesses, and any other options will be key. Connect by networking with people you know in your community. Talk to other parents. Anything you can do, do it for the success of your child.

How Long Do You Anticipate Your Child Staying Home With You After High School?

As we know, parenting requires work, and if you do not invest time and energy in your child, this could affect how long your child will stay in your household. Follow the steps for creating a career plan, and consult with your child about a timeline with an anticipation date for when your child will be leaving home. For those kids who need more structure and extra guidance, this plan will be very important. Not having a plan in place could delay your child from leaving the nest.

Leaving the Nest: It's Hard to Let Go

Speaking about children leaving the nest can be difficult for some parents. You bonded with your children, you had ups and downs, but in the end things always worked out. Now it's time for them to leave home. When children move on to the next chapter in their lives some parents may experience a feeling of abandonment. We don't expect our children to live at home forever, but it can still be a difficult process for some parents. Remember to seek the support of your family, friends, counselors, and community to help you through this time.

As a parent, you have completed a journey with your child, and now your child has left the nest. If there are other children in the home, it is always helpful to reflect on your parenting skills to see if there is something different you should consider

doing with the other siblings. Here is a "Parenting

Reflection Journal."

Parenting Reflection Journal:
What's Next?

Career Interests:

_____

_____

_____

Activities
(Academics/Athletics/Sports/DECA/Music):

_____

_____

_____

Community Service Projects (Places to Volunteer):

_____

_____

_____

Review Plan (College/Military/Tech School/Job):

_____

_____

_____

College Entrance Exams (SAT/PSAT/ACT):

_____

_____

_____

Parenting Reflection Journal:
Leaving the Nest

Is there a positive plan in place for my child(ren) to leave the nest?

_____

_____

_____

Short-term goals:

_____

_____

_____

Long-term goals:

_____

_____

_____

Is there more I can do as a parent to support my child(ren)?

_____

_____

_____

_____

_____

_____

_____

_____

_____

CHAPTER 10: REFLECTING ON YOUR PARENTING JOURNEY

There are many journeys we ALL will take in life, and one of the biggest ones will be the one we take with our children. Our children are only with us for a short period of time. Before you know it, they are off into the world. What we do to prepare them for this is truly important. Valuable time must be spent in building strong family bonds and relationships with our kids. They will always remember those precious moments, so do your best to create them.

Final Thoughts

Being supported by my parents and showing support when I became a parent to my daughter helped me to understand my parents' hard work. I was very fortunate to have a child who continually kept busy with positive school activities and community service projects. Teaching and modeling for her how to give back to others in the community at an early age really helped to shape who she has become today. My hope is that this book will help some parents with student success. The ride may be bumpy with your child, but stay the course and stay on the ride and it could be fun in the end. You will have so much to talk about that ride in later years.

"People don't care how much you know until they know

how much you care."

John C. Maxwell

"Find out who you are, and do it on purpose."

Dolly Parton

"The real innovators did their innovating by just

being themselves."

Count Basie

REFERENCES

Baumrind, D. (1966). Effects of authoritative parental control on child behavior, *Child Development, 37*(4), 887–907.

Baumrind, D. (1971). Harmonious parents and their preschool children. *Developmental Psychology, 4*(1), 99–102.

Baumrind, D. (1991). Parenting styles and adolescent development. In R. Lerner, A. C. Peterson, and J. Brooks-Gunn (Eds.), *Encyclopedia of Adolescence*, vol. 2 (pp. 746–758). New York, NY: Garland.

Greenspan, S. (1978). Maternal affect-allowance and limit-setting appropriateness as predictors of child adjustment. *Genetic Psychology Monographs, 98*(1), 83–111.

Greenspan, S. (1985). An integrative model of caregiver discipline. *Child Care Quarterly, 14*(1), 30–47.

Lyon, G. E. (1999). Where I'm from. In *Where I'm From: Where Poems Come From* (pp. 3–4). Spring, TX: Absey & Co.

Parenting. (n.d.). In *Merriam-Webster's Dictionary*. Retrieved from http://www.merriam-webster.com

Made in the USA
Charleston, SC
12 August 2015